My First Book About

HORSES and PONIES

By Kama Einhorn

Illustrated by Christopher Moroney

Random House 🏠 New York

Giddy-up! It is I, Professor Grover, here with my trusted sidekick, Elmo. Elmo loves riding his rocking horse and his hobbyhorse and playing with his toy horses. So I, Professor Grover, thought that Elmo might like to learn all about REAL horses and ponies.

Let us follow the galloping horse on the next page into the book. Will you come along for the ride? If your answer is yes, just say giddy-up. You said it! Oh, good. Then hi-ho and let us go!

Horses
&
Ponies

But first, here is some very important advice about horses: If you want to meet a horse, you must make sure you are with a grown-up. Adults who work in stables, where some horses live, know each horse and how it behaves around new people. Most horses are calm and gentle, but some horses are nervous around people and might kick. And there are some horses that do not want to be ridden.

There are many different breeds, or kinds, of horses.

Horses come in different sizes and different colors, and some breeds are mostly found in specific countries.

Horsehair can be any combination of brown, black, red, white, gray, or spotted.

quarter horses

Shetland ponies

Appaloosa

Ponies are a smaller kind of horse. They have thicker coats, shorter legs, thick necks, short heads with broad foreheads, and thick manes and tails.

Shire horses

The world record for the biggest horse was a Shire horse called Mammoth. By the time he was four years old, he was more than seven feet tall! That's as tall as a very tall basketball player!

mane
withers
tail
muzzle
hock
fetlock
hoof

paint horse

Now THAT is what I would call a horse of a different color!

Bay
Chestnut
Palomino
Roan
Dun
Pinto
Appaloosa
Black
White
Gray

A baby horse is called a foal.

Male foals are called colts. Female foals are called fillies.

Most foals are born at night because the darkness protects them from danger.

Spring is the best time of year for a foal to be born. The weather is nice and warm and there's lots of grass for the mother to eat.

Newborn foals do not eat grass. Their legs are so long they can't reach it! For the first few months, a foal gets all the food it needs from its mother's milk.

mare and colt

Within an hour of being born, a foal is able to stand up and walk. It takes most human babies at least a whole year to walk!

Arabian foal

A foal's legs are almost the length of a full-grown horse's. So, while a foal's body will get a lot bigger over time, its legs are already almost as long as they will be when it grows up.

Wow, they don't horse around!

yearlings

A yearling is a horse between the ages of one and two.

Male yearlings grow into stallions, and female yearlings grow into mares.

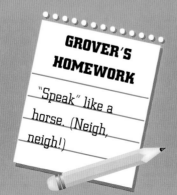

GROVER'S HOMEWORK

"Speak" like a horse. (Neigh, neigh!)

Horses have long, large heads and big mouths.

A horse's teeth grow all the time, just like fingernails. They get worn down by chewing. As a horse gets older, its teeth get longer and more yellow.

GROVER'S HOMEWORK

Count the teeth that you see in this horse's mouth. How many teeth do you have in **YOUR** mouth?

Horses eat hay and grass. They also eat alfalfa, barley, oats, corn, molasses, vegetables, fruits, and sugar. To feed a horse safely, put a treat in your flat, open palm and let the horse take it.

A horse has eyes on the sides of its head so it can see all around without having to move its head very much.

Yum, yum. So there you have it. Straight from the horse's mouth.

Peruvian Pa

Horses toss their manes (and swish their tails) to shoo away annoying bugs.

Horses hear better than people do. They have big ears, which they can move around and point toward a sound.

Horses also have a better sense of smell than humans. Their long heads have lots of room for their sensitive noses.

TWIDDLEBUG TRIVIA

A horse's tail is very important: Not only is it used to swat flies, but it also keeps a horse's bottom warm in cold weather!

Many horses have white markings on their faces.

◆ A star (which is really a diamond shape) is found between the eyes.

▪ A stripe is a long, straight mark that goes down the nose.

▪ A blaze is a broad mark that goes down the front of the face.

● A snip is a small mark on the muzzle, or tip of the nose.

Shoo, fly. Don't bother Grover or Elmo!

Horses have big, strong bodies. They have four long legs that enable them to run and jump easily.

The fastest reco[rd] speed of any ho[rse] is 43 miles per h[our]. That's almost as fast as cars go on a highway!

Horses move in lots of different ways and at different speeds. These movements are called **gaits.** From slowest to fastest, these gaits are called **walk, trot, canter,** and **gallop.** When a horse gallops, its four hooves all come off the ground at the same time.

galloping

Hoof clipping doesn't hurt the horse, just like it doesn't hurt to cut your fingernails or to put on shoes.

A horse's hooves are a little bit like your fingernails. Both are mad[e] of something called **keratin.** Hooves are always growing, so ma[ny] horses need to have them trimme[d]. And they need to wear shoes to protect their hooves and feet!

Horseshoes keep a horse's hoov[es] from cracking. A person who clips hooves and fits them for shoes is called a **farrier.**

When a horse stands on its hind, or back, legs, it is "rearing up." Horses can also use their hooves to kick.

Do you want to learn more? All righty, then, let us hoof it to the next page!

A horseshoe is considered a symbol of good luck. People hang them up over their doors to bring good fortune. The horseshoe must hang with the open side facing skyward so the luck doesn't "spill out"!

Many years ago, horsehair was used as a stuffing for sofas and mattresses. It's hard and scratchy, so it didn't make very comfortable cushioning!

GROVER'S HOMEWORK

Get up and move around like a horse.

Horses have helped people for thousands of years. That's much longer ago than anyone can remember.

cave drawing of a horse

Drawings of horses that have been found in caves tell us that horses and people have been living together for a long, long time.

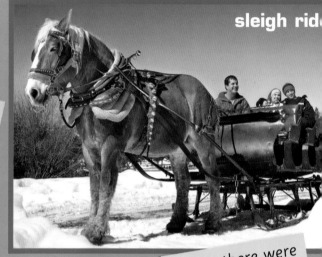

sleigh rid[e]

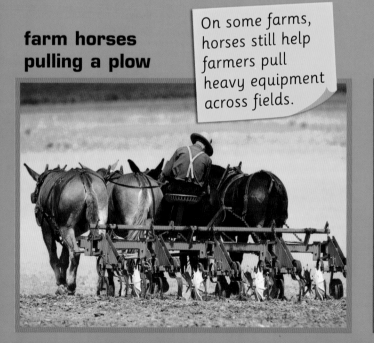

farm horses pulling a plow

On some farms, horses still help farmers pull heavy equipment across fields.

horse-drawn carriage

Before there were cars, people used horse-drawn vehicles to get around.

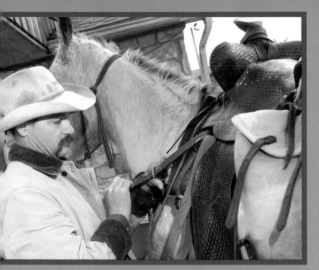

Cowboy preparing to ride a horse

Horses are still used to herd, or gather, animals on a farm.

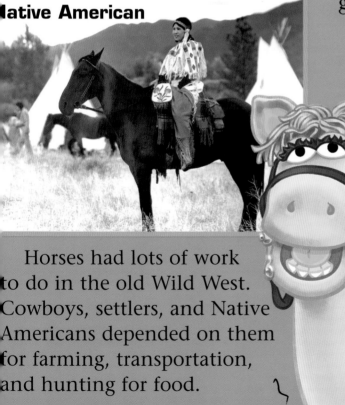

Native American

Horses had lots of work to do in the old Wild West. Cowboys, settlers, and Native Americans depended on them for farming, transportation, and hunting for food.

Horses still help people in many ways.

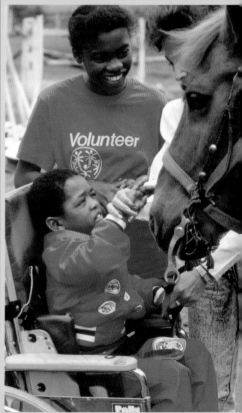

Horses can help people with disabilities keep their muscles strong. This is called **equine therapy.** They can help people learn balance, coordination, trust, and patience.

In the United States, people keep horses mostly to have fun with them, to ride them, and to take care of them.

It takes a lot of time, patience, and understanding to learn to take care of and train horses. A person must be kind and gentle to a horse, and keep it clean, watered, and well fed. A strong bond of affection and trust can grow between a horse and the person who owns and takes care of it.

Just as you do on a bicycle or roller skates, you must always wear a helmet when riding a horse to protect your head in case you fall.

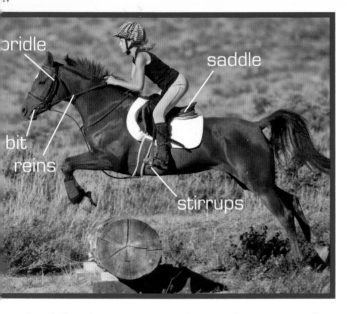

bridle
saddle
bit
reins
stirrups

People use special equipment to ride a horse. The **bridle** is the headgear that lets a rider tell a horse how to move. A bridle has **reins** and a **bit.** The bit fits in the horse's mouth. Usually, a rider sits in a **saddle** and holds the reins. The rider uses the reins to tell the horse what to do—to stop or go or turn. **Stirrups** hang from the saddle and hold the rider's feet.

People who train horses may take them to shows and competitions, where both riders and horses are judged on the way they ride together.

These horses have prize ribbons on their bridles.

Now you know a lot about horses. But there are still some surprises.

Congratulations. You have now completed the "Horse Course"! You have worked very hard to learn about horses—you are a regular workhorse! But, oh—lookie here. There is still more to discover.

Horses sleep standing up. Their legs "lock" and then they go into a light sleep. Sometimes, if they feel safe, horses will sleep lying down.

Horses have large hearts and strong lungs to help them run fast. A horse's heart weighs as much as 16 human hearts.

Something else you may want to know is how a person takes care of a horse.

Horses 101

All horses need:
Food and fresh water
Space to move around outside
Exercise every day
The companionship of other horses or animals like goats
A safe place to sleep
Grooming, such as brushing, bathing, and hoof care
Veterinary care (a veterinarian is a doctor who takes care of animals)

Wild horses still exist in a number of places around the world. These untamed horses are remnants of much larger herds that roamed free in wide-open spaces. But uninhabited areas are shrinking, which is a big problem for these horses. Happily, a number of conservation groups now work to ensure that these proud creatures remain free and safe in protected habitats.

wild horses in snow

Zebras and donkeys are related to horses.

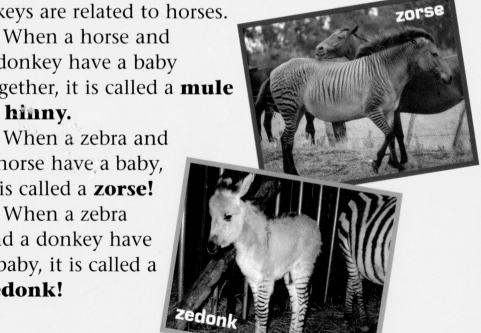
zorse

When a horse and a donkey have a baby together, it is called a **mule** or **hinny.**

When a zebra and a horse have a baby, it is called a **zorse!**

When a zebra and a donkey have a baby, it is called a **zedonk!**

mule

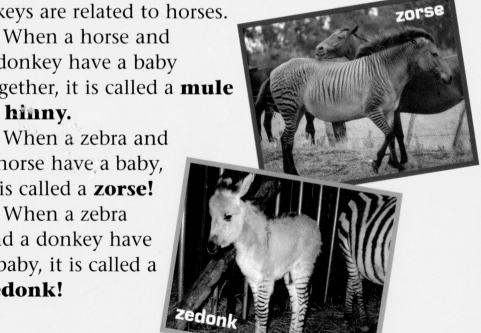
zedonk

"EXTRA-CREDIT" FUN FOR EVERYONE!

If you want to learn more about horses and ponies, here are some things you can do with your family:

1. Visit a local stable. The people who work there may be able to show you the horses, and how they are fed and cared for, and where they exercise. If you want to learn to take care of and ride a horse yourself, many stables give lessons. Riding stables can be found in or near many towns and even in most big cities.

2. Horses are measured in "hands." A hand, in horse measurement, is four inches. Measure the height of something like a table in hands. How many hands high is your table? Measure the people in your family. Who is the most hands high?

3. Create a horse scrapbook. Collect pictures of different breeds. What can you learn about each type of horse that is special to that type?

4. Visit a zoo to see some horse "cousins"—zebras, rhinoceroses, and tapirs. How do they look similar to horses? How do they look different?